VALLEY 10/12/2010 C:1
5069001
Thoreau
Thumbing through Thoreau
:
a book of quotations by

VALLEY COMMUNITY LIBRARY
739 RIVER STREET
PECKVILLE, PA 18452
(570) 489-1765
www.lclshome.org

THUMBING THROUGH
THOREAU
A Book of Quotations by Henry David Thoreau

Valley Community Library
739 River Street
Peckville, PA 18452-2313

Copyright © 2010 Kenny Luck, Jay Luke & Ren Adams

Except for the use of short passages for review purposes, no part of this book may be reproduced, in part or in whole, or transmitted in any form or by any means, electronically or mechanically, including photocopying, recording, or any information or storage retrieval system, without prior permission in writing from the publisher.

First Edition 2010
Printed in the United States of America

Cover image: reproduced from the original watercolor painting, *Woodland Visitors* by Nicholas P. Santoleri © 1993
Cover designer: Patrick Tigranian
Interior designer: James Arneson
Interior illustrations (even numbered pages): Jay Luke
Interior illustrations (odd numbered pages): Ren Adams

ISBN: 978-0-9822565-4-1
Library of Congress Control Number: 2010926175

Tribute Books
PO Box 95
Archbald, Pennsylvania 18403
(570) 876-2416
Email: info@tribute-books.com
Website: www.tribute-books.com

For information on bulk purchase discounts or for fundraising opportunities, please contact the special sales division of Tribute Books at: info@tribute-books.com

Visit www.ThumbingThroughThoreau.com and email Kenny Luck at kenny@tribute-books.com

Publisher's Cataloging-in-Publication data

Thoreau, Henry David, 1817-1862.
　　Thumbing through Thoreau: a book of quotations by Henry David Thoreau/compiled by Kenny Luck; illustrated by Jay Luke and Ren Adams.
　　　p. cm.
　　Includes bibliographical references and index.
　　ISBN 978-0-9822565-4-1
1. Thoreau, Henry David, 1817-1862 –Quotations. 2. Quotations, American. 3. Nature –Quotations, maxims, etc. 4. Spirituality –Quotations, maxims, etc. 5. United States –Politics and government –Quotations, maxims, etc. 6. Love –Quotations, maxims, etc. I. Luck, Kenny. II. Luke, Jay. III. Adams, Ren. IV. Title.

PS3042 .L83 2010
818/.309–dc22   2010926175

THUMBING THROUGH
THOREAU

A Book of Quotations by Henry David Thoreau

Compiled by KENNY LUCK
Illustrated by JAY LUKE and REN ADAMS

Dedication

This book is dedicated to the following wonderful women … *thank you!*

Barbra Hoffman (1943-2007)
you gave me wings and taught me to fly

Alena Vauter
my love, life and muse

Dr. Ann Bush
for your continued encouragement and support

Dr. Kathleen Munley
for your professional and personal guidance

Darcy Ford
for all of the laughter and joy you bring

Nicole Langan
for your hard work, ideas and belief in this project

Contents

Introduction..ix

Section I
Society & Government..1

Section II
Spirituality & Nature..87

Section III
Love...271

Index..297

Bibliography...301

Acknowledgments...303

Cover Painting...305

Introduction ❦

> *"If I were to be baptized it should be in this pond,"* wrote Nathanial Hawthorne, *reflecting upon the majesty of Walden Pond one autumn afternoon in 1843. "But then one would not wish to pollute it by washing off his sins into it. None but angels should bathe here."*

As I stood on the edge of Walden Pond, about to make a symbolic leap into what had become in my mind a scared place, Hawthorne's poetic observation was not present in my thoughts. For a summer day, it was unusually cold; a light mist rose above the surface of the water; and having forgotten my towel and bathing suit at home in Pennsylvania, I was forced to strip down, making do with what I was wearing in that revealing moment. I hung my clothes on a nearby tree branch and began inching my way toward the water. It was a ritual Henry David Thoreau, one of America's first literary giants, had performed countless times during his stay in the woods.

It was June 2007, and this was my second trip to Walden Pond. I had visited the previous summer but resolved only to walk along the shoreline, avoiding the seduction of the water. "This time," I thought to myself, "I am going in." Although I was initially reluctant, once the water rose past by waistline, I felt an extraordinary release. I made one final push off the rock where I was standing and let go. I let the water take me. Feeling free from constraints, I had transformed into one of Hawthorne's angels, baptized by the clear, cool waters of the pond.

My experience at Walden Pond that day was emblematic. It was the culmination of a two-year journey which led me to Concord, Massachusetts, where I hoped to retrace the steps of a man who I had never met, but felt an extraordinary affinity towards. Moreover, I saw a little bit of myself in Thoreau. Here was a man who, despite the conventions of his day, shunned every comfort and convenience. Thoreau once refused to take a doormat, for instance, offered to him by an elderly woman, hoping to avoid what he called the "beginnings of evil." It seemed like something I would have done had I not read about it first. For the first time in my young life, I met my literary and intellectual soul mate.

Approaching Thoreau from a devotional, rather than an academic point of view, I began collecting short quotes from his works for my own purposes. Most of the quote collecting occurred in the winter months of 2006, when I was a third year undergraduate student. I spent countless hours in my university library between classes pouring over thousands of pages. I cherished each quote and in a short time was able to recite long passages from memory. Commenting on society, nature, government, spirituality and love, there seemed to be a Thoreau quote for every season. After roughly one month my list had expanded into a plethora of pages. Then, I got an idea: Why not share these treasures with others? And so it began.

Choosing which quotes to include and which quotes to ignore is tricky. With the aim of trying to preserve Thoreau's original intentions, I was careful to not take any passage out of context. No precedent can dictate the proper course of action. However, Thoreau's lyrical writing style makes it easy to find short, memorable truisms. Much of his best work lay not in the familiar, but in the unfamiliar. As a dedicated diarist, he wrote incessantly nearly every day. I found that the wisdom contained in his journal entries rivaled the most complex systems of thought laid out by any philosopher before or since. His correspondences, particularly with Harrison Blake, are even more exceptional. As the two men swapped letters between one another, Thoreau always found new ways to transform even the most mundane subjects into brilliant pieces of insight.

This book, appropriate for the beginner or devotee, is my attempt to bring together the best pieces of Thoreau's writings in one collection. It is the result of long hours of hard work by several people, and a determination constantly fueled by one inspiring idea: "If one advances confidently in the direction of his dreams, and endeavors to live the life which he has imagined," Thoreau wrote in the closing of Walden, "he will meet with a success unexpected in common hours." In the end, we could all use a dose of Thoreau from time to time.

Kenny Luck
April 2010

Kenny Luck visiting Henry David Thoreau's grave (October 2006).

SECTION I
Society & Government

I should not talk so much about **myself** if there were anybody else whom I **knew** as **well.**

(*Walden*, "Economy," p. 4)

Most men, even in this comparatively free country, through mere ignorance and mistake, are so occupied with the factitious cares and superfluously coarse labors of life that its finer fruits cannot be plucked by them.

(*Walden*, "Economy," p. 6)

He has no time to be anything but a machine.

(*Walden*, "Economy," p. 6)

The mass of men lead lives of quiet desperation.

(*Walden*, "Economy," p. 8)

It is never too late to give up our prejudices.

(*Walden*, "Economy," p. 9)

Most of the **luxuries**, and many of the so-called comforts of life, are not only not **indispensable, but positive hindrances to** the elevation to mankind. With respect **to luxuries and comforts, the wisest have** ever lived a more simple and meager life **than the poor. The ancient philosophers,** Chinese, Hind[u], Persian, and Greeks, were a **class than which none has been poorer in** outward riches, none so rich inward.

(*Walden*, "Economy," p. 15)

The **philosopher** is in advance of his age even in the **outward form** of his life. He is not fed, sheltered, clothed, warmed, like his **contemporaries.**

(*Walden,* "Economy," p. 16)

I say, be aware of all enterprises that **require** new clothes, and not rather a new **wearer** of clothes.

(*Walden*, "Economy," p. 26)

While civilization has been improving our houses, it has not equally improved the men who are to inhabit them.

(*Walden*, "Economy," p. 37)

Men have become tools of their tools.

(*Walden*, "Economy," p. 41)

Section I: Society & Government

We are in **great haste** to construct a **magnetic telegraph** from Maine to Texas; but Maine and Texas, **it may be,** having **nothing important** to communicate.

(*Walden*, "Economy," p. 58)

Man is an **animal** who more than any other can **adapt** himself to **all** climates and circumstances.

(*Walden*, "Economy," p. 70)

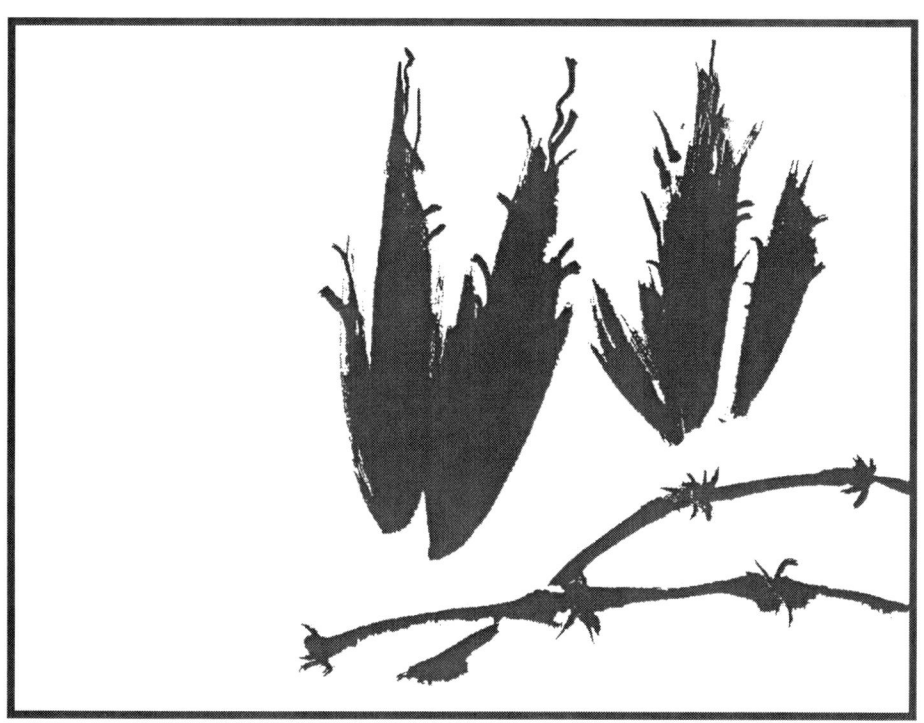

Section I: Society & Government / 13

A lady once offered me a mat, but as I had **no room** to spare within the house, **nor time** to spare within the house, I declined it, preferring to wipe my **feet** on the sod before my **door**. It is best to avoid the **beginnings of evil**.

(*Walden*, "Economy," p. 74)

Above all, as I have implied, the **man** who goes **alone** can start today; but he who travels with **another** must **wait** 'til the other is ready, and it may be a **long time** before they get off.

(*Walden*, "Economy," p. 80)

...for a rich man is rich in proportion to the number of things he can afford to let alone.

(*Walden*, "Where I've Lived," p. 91)

I have found thus that **I had been a rich man** without any damage to **my poverty.**

(*Walden*, "Where I've Lived," p. 91)

To a **philosopher** all **news**, as it is called, is **gossip**, and they who edit and read it are **old women** over their tea.

(*Walden*, "Where I've Lived," pp. 104-105)

Children, who play life, **discern its true law** and relations more **clearly** than men, **who fail to live it worthily**, but who think that they are wiser by experience, that is, **by failure.**

(*Walden*, "Where I've Lived," p. 106)

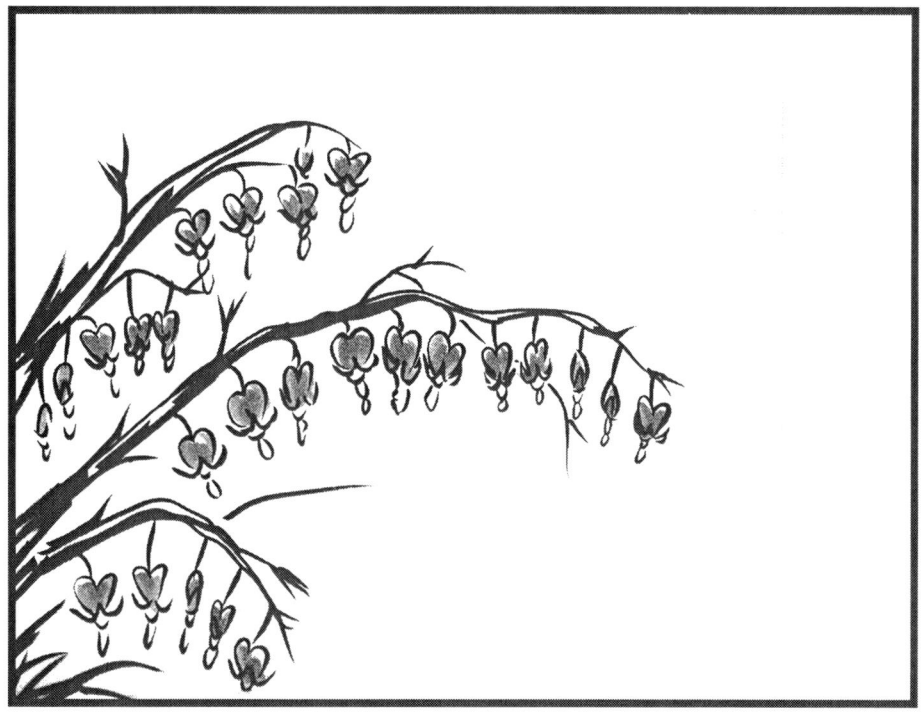

Section I: Society & Government / 19

Most men are **satisfied** if they read or hear read, **and perchance have been convicted** by the wisdom of **one good book**, the **Bible,** and for the rest of their **lives** vegetate and **dissipate** their faculties in what is called **easy reading.**

(*Walden*, "Reading," p. 116)

It is not **all books** that are as **dull** as their **readers.**

(*Walden*, "Reading," p. 119)

Section I: Society & Government / 21

I had **three chairs** in my house; one for solitude, two for friendship, three for society.

(*Walden*, "Visitors," p. 155)

I am convinced, that if all men were to live as simply as I then did, thieving and robbery would be unknown.

(*Walden*, "The Village," p. 191)

It is remarkable **how long men** will believe the **bottomlessness** of a **pond** without taking the **trouble** to sound it.

(*Walden*, "The Pond in Winter," p. 315)

It is not for a man to put himself in such an **attitude to society,** but to maintain himself in whatever attitude he finds himself through obedience to the laws of his being, which will never be one of **opposition to a just government**, if he should **chance to meet** with such.

(*Walden*, "Conclusion," p. 355)

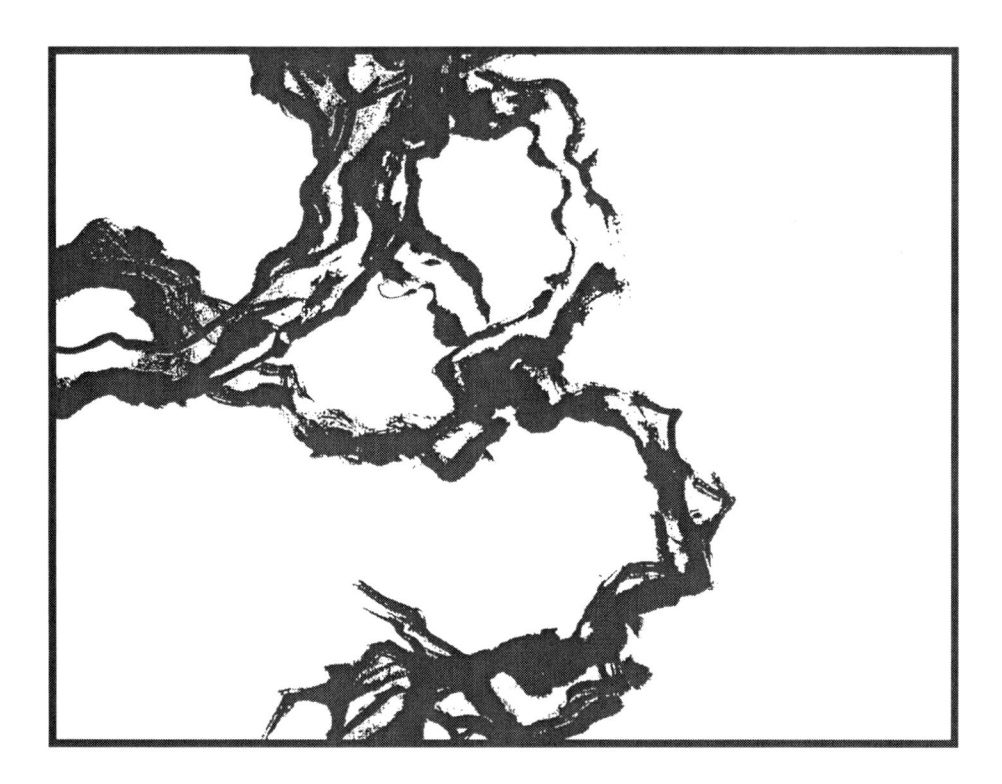

How **worn and dusty,** then, must be the **highways of the world** – how deep **the ruts** of tradition **and conformity!**

(*Walden*, "Conclusion," p. 356)

Superfluous **wealth** can buy superfluities **only.** Money is **not** required to **buy** one necessary of **the soul.**

(*Walden*, "Conclusion," p. 362)

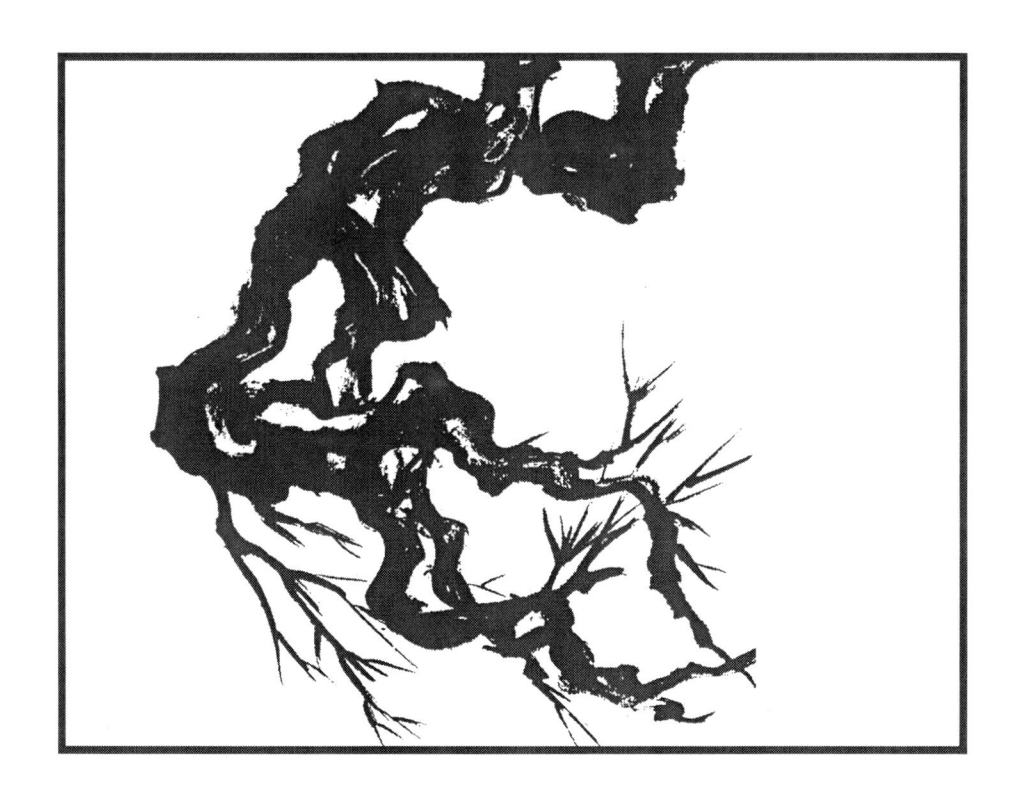

… [the] government is **best** which governs least; and I should like to see it acted up to more **rapidly and systematically.** Carried out, it finally amounts to this, **which also I believe –** that government is best which governs not at all; **and when men are prepared for it,** that will be the kind of government **which they will have.**

(*Civil Disobedience*, p. 356)

Let every man make known **what kind of government** would command his respect, **and that will be one step closer to obtaining it.**

(*Civil Disobedience*, p. 357)

Must the **citizen** ever for a moment, or in the least degree, **resign his conscience to the legislature?** Why has every man a conscience, then? I think we should be men first, and **subjects afterward.**

(*Civil Disobedience*, p. 358)

I cannot for an instant recognize that **political organization** as my government which is the slave's government also.

(*Civil Disobedience*, p. 360)

Section I: Society & Government / 31

All men recognize the right to **revolution;** that is, the right to refuse allegiance to, **and to resist,** the government, when **its tyranny** or its **inefficiency** are great and unendurable.

(*Civil Disobedience*, p. 360)

There are **thousands** who are in opinion **opposed to slavery** and to the war, who yet in effect do nothing to put **an end** to them ...

(*Civil Disobedience*, p. 362)

Section I: Society & Government / 33

I cast my vote, perchance, as I think right; but I am not vitally concerned that right should prevail ... A wise man will not leave the right to the mercy of chance, nor wish it to prevail through the power of the majority.

(*Civil Disobedience*, p. 363)

Unjust laws exist: shall we be content to obey them, **or shall we endeavor** to **amend** them, and obey them until we have succeeded, **or shall we transgress** them at once?

(*Civil Disobedience*, p. 367)

… if it [the law] is of such a nature that it requires you to be the agent of injustice to another, then, I say, break the law.

(*Civil Disobedience*, p. 368)

Moreover, any man **more right** than his neighbors **constitutes a majority** of one already.

(*Civil Disobedience*, p. 369)

Section I: Society & Government

A minority is **powerless** while it conforms to the majority; **it is not even** a minority then; **but it is irresistible** when it clogs by its whole weight.

(*Civil Disobedience*, p. 371)

If a thousand men were not to pay their tax-bills this year, that would not be a violent and bloody measure, as it would be to pay them, and enable that State to commit violence and shed innocent blood. This is, in fact, the definition of a peaceful revolution, if any such is possible.

(*Civil Disobedience*, p. 371)

... **the rich man** – not to make any invidious comparison – **is always sold to the institution** which makes him rich. Absolutely speaking, **the more money, the less virtue**; for money comes between a man and his objects, and obtains them for him; and it was certainly **no great virtue** to obtain it.

(*Civil Disobedience*, p. 372)

The best thing a man can do **for his culture** when he is **rich** is to endeavor to carry out **those schemes** which he entertained when **he was poor.**

(*Civil Disobedience*, p. 372)

Seen from a lower point of view, the Constitution, with all its faults, is very good; the law and the courts are very respectful; even this State and this American government are, in many respects, very admirable and rare things, to be thankful for, such as a great many have described them; but seen from a point of view a little higher, they are what I described them; seen from a higher still, and the highest, who shall say what they are, or that they are worth looking at or thinking of at all?

(*Civil Disobedience*, p. 383)

... **the government** does not concern me much, and I shall bestow the **fewest possible thoughts** on it.

(*Civil Disobedience*, p. 383)

Section I: Society & Government

No man with a genius for legislation has appeared in America. They are rare in the history of the world.

(*Civil Disobedience*, p. 386)

There will never be a really free and enlightened State until the State comes to recognize the individual as a higher and independent power, from which all its own power and authority are derived, and treats him accordingly.

(*Civil Disobedience*, p. 387)

If a man does not keep pace with his companions, perhaps it is because he hears a different drummer. Let him step to the music which he hears, however measured or far away.

(*Walden*, "Conclusion," p. 358)

... the State never intentionally confronts a man's sense, **intellectual or moral,** but only his body, his senses. It is not armed with superior wit or honesty, but with superior **physical strength.**

(*Civil Disobedience*, p. 376)

There is but little virtue in the action of masses of men.

(*Civil Disobedience*, p. 363)

By myself I can live
and thrive, but in the society of
incompatible friends I starve.

(Journal V, vol. II, April 2, 1853, pp. 86-87)

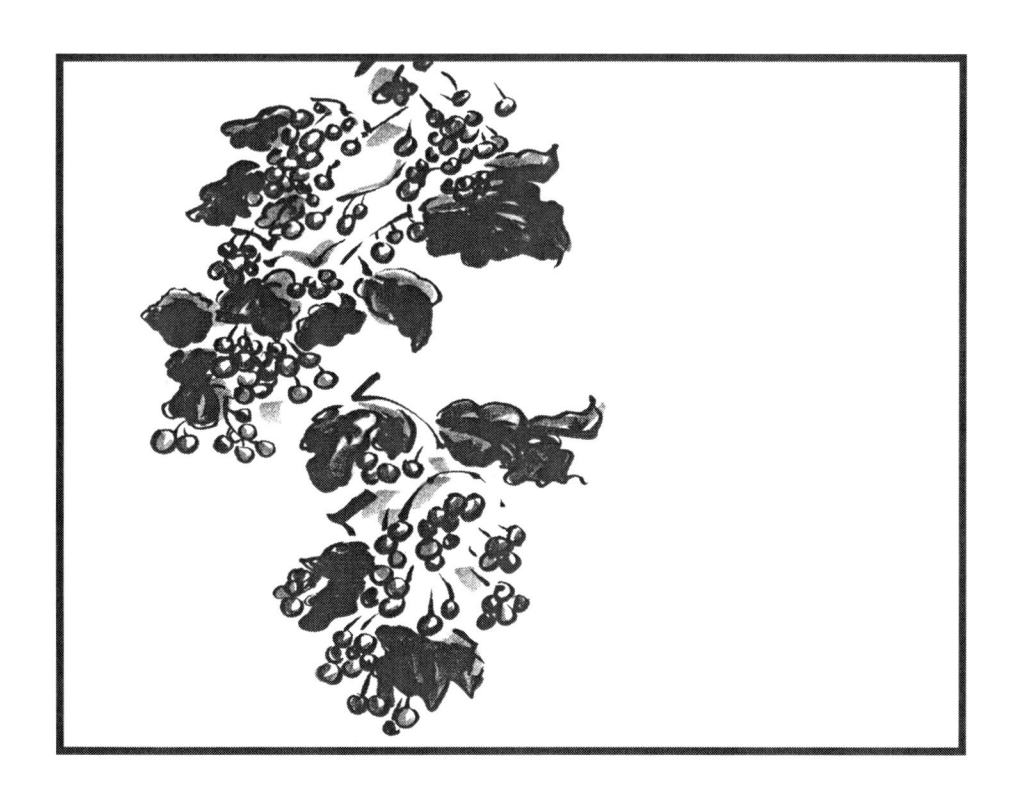

How **many men** meet with some blast in the moist growing days of their **youth,** and what should have been a **sweet and palatable fruit in them** becomes a mere puff and excrescence, ripening no kernel, and they say that they have experienced religion!

(Journal V, vol. II, June 1, 1853, p. 210)

The mass of mankind, who live in houses or shops ... know nothing of the **beautiful days** which are passing about and around them. Is not such a day worthy of a hymn? It is such a day as mankind might spend in praising and glorifying nature. It might be spent as a natural Sabbath, if only all men would accept the hint, devoted to unworthy thoughts.
(Journal V, vol. II, August 19, 1853, p. 383)

The savage lives **simply** through ignorance and idleness or laziness, but the philosopher lives simply through wisdom. In the case of the **savage,** the accompaniment of simplicity is idleness with its attendant **vices,** but in the case of the philosopher, it is the **highest** employment and development ... There are two kinds of **simplicity** – one that is akin to foolishness, the other to **wisdom**. The philosopher's style of living is only outwardly simple, but inwardly **complex**. The savage's style is both **outwardly and inwardly simple.**

(Journal V, vol. II, September 1, 1853, pp. 410-412)

A **simpleton** can perform many **mechanical labors,** but it is not capable of **profound thought.**

(Journal V, vol. II, September 1, 1853, p. 412)

So much do we love actions that are **simple.** They are all **poetic.** We, too, would fain be so employed. So unlike the pursuits of most men, so **artificial** or complicated.

(Journal V, vol. II, October 22, 1853, p. 444)

For if I buy one necessary of life, I cheat myself to some extent, I deprive myself of the pleasure, the inexpressible joy, which is the unfailing reward of satisfying any want of our nature simply and truly.

(Journal V, vol. II, October 22, 1853, p. 445)

Wealth cannot buy a man a home **in Nature-house** or farm there.

(Journal V, vol. II, November 11, 1853, p. 497)

It is **astonishing** as well as **sad,** how many **trivial affairs** even the wisest man thinks he **must attend to** in a day …

(*Familiar Letters and Index vol.6*, "Letter to Harrison Blake," March 27, 1848, p. 161)

There is **not one** kind of food for **all** men.

(*Familiar Letters and Index* vol. 6, "Letter to Harrison Blake," May 2, 1848, p. 165)

It is true actually as it is true really; it is true materially as it is true spiritually, that they who seek honestly and sincerely, with all their hearts and lives and strength, to earn their bread, do earn it, and it is sure to be very sweet to them.

(*Familiar Letters and Index* vol. 6, "Letter to Harrison Blake," May 2, 1848, p. 165)

If I were to **consciously** join any **party,** it would be that which is the most free to entertain **thought.**

(*Familiar Letters and Index vol. 6*, "Letter to Harrison Blake," July 21, 1852, p. 190)

A **wise man** is as unconscious of the movements of the **body politic** as he is of the process of digestion and the circulation of the blood in his **natural body.**

(Journal III, vol. 9, November 9, 1851, p. 103)

If it were not for **death** and **funerals,** I think the **institution** of the **church** would **stand** no longer.

(Journal III, vol. 9, November 16, 1851, p. 120)

We must have infinite faith in each other. If we have not, we must never let it leak out that we have not.

(Journal III, vol. 9, January 31, 1852, p. 258)

Not the same things are great to all men.

(Journal III, vol. 9, January 31, 1852, p. 258)

There are some things which **God** may afford to **smile** at; men **cannot.**

(Journal III, vol. 9, February 1, 1852, p. 267)

It is hard for a man to take money from his friends ... This suggests how all men should be related.

(Journal III, vol. 9, April 11, 1852, p. 401)

A companion can possess **no worse** quality than **vulgarity.**

(Journal III, vol. 9, April 12, 1852, p. 407)

The vast majority are **men of society. They live on the surface;** they are interested in the **transient** and fleeting; **they are like driftwood on the flood** … They have **no knowledge** of truth, **but by an exceeding dim and transient instinct,** **which stereotypes** the church and some other institutions.

(Journal III, vol. 9, April 24, 1852, p. 460)

It is impossible for me to be interested in what interests **men** generally. Their pursuits and interests seem to me frivolous ... These affairs of men are so narrow as to afford **no vista,** no distance; it is a shallow foreground only, **no large extended views to be taken.**

(Journal III, vol. 9, April 24, 1852, p. 461)

Men talk of freedom! How many are free to think ... No exercise implies more real manhood and **vigor** than joining thought to thought. How few men can tell what they have thought!

(Journal X, vol. 16, May 6, 1858, pp. 404-405)

The mass never comes up to the **standard** of its best member, but on the contrary degrades itself to a level with the **lowest** ... Hence the mass is **only another name for the mob.**

(Journal I, vol. 7, March 14, 1838, p. 36)

A true poem is not that which the public read. There is always a poem not printed on paper, coincident with the production of this, which is stereotyped in the poet's life, is what he has become through his work.

(Journal I, vol. 7, July 1, 1840, p. 157)

Nothing was ever so **unfamiliar** and **startling** to me as my own thoughts … All a man's privacy is in his eye, and its expression **he cannot alter** more than he can alter **his character.**

(Journal I, vol. 7, July 10, 1840, p. 166)

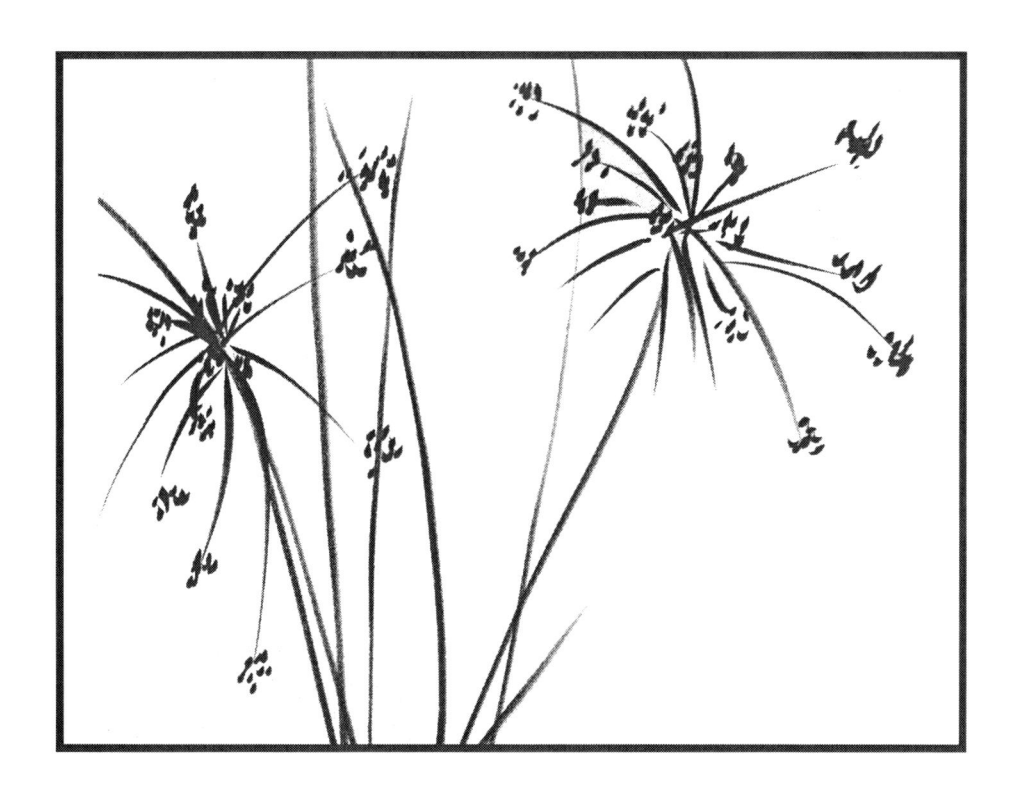

At each **step** man measures himself **against** the system.

(Journal I, vol. 7, January 31, 1841, p. 188)

Those great men who are unknown to their own **generation** are **already famous** in the society of the great who have **gone before** them. **All worldly fame** but subsides from their high estimate beyond **the stars.**

(Journal I, vol. 7, February 12, 1841, pp. 212-213)

Nothing can be more useful to a man than a **determination** not to be hurried.

(Journal I, vol. 7, March 22, 1842, p. 342)

We know each other **better** than we are aware; we are admitted to **startling privacies** with every person we meet, and in some **emergency** we shall find how well we knew him.

(Journal I, vol. 7, March 30, 1842, p. 356)

The heroes and discoverers have found true more than was previously believed, only when they were expecting and dreaming of something more than their contemporaries dreamed of ...

(Journal II, vol. 8, 1850, p. 11)

We inspire friendship in men when we have contracted friendship with the gods.

(Journal II, vol. 8, June 1850, p. 33)

Every man carries a fire in his **eye,** or in **his** blood, or in his **brain.**

(Journal II, vol. 8, July 16, 1850, p. 41)

What does **education** often do? It makes a straight-cut **ditch** of a free, meandering **brook.**

(Journal II, vol. 8, 1850, p. 83)

What is it [to] be born **free and equal**, and not to live? What is the value of any **political freedom**, but as a means to **moral** freedom?

(Journal II, vol. 8, February 16, 1851, p. 162)

Of two men, one of whom knows **nothing** about a subject, and, what is extremely **rare,** knows that he knows nothing, and the other really **knows** something about it, but **thinks** that he knows all – what great advantage has the latter over the former?

(Journal II, vol. 8, February 27, 1851, p. 167)

Obey the law which reveals, **and not** the **law** revealed.

(Journal II, vol. 8, 1851, p. 171)

The way in which men cling to old institutions after the life has departed out of them, and out of themselves, reminds me of those monkeys which cling by their tails ... whose tails contract about their limbs, even the dead limbs, of the forest, and they hang suspended beyond the hunters reach long after they are dead. It is no use to argue with such men.

(Journal II, vol. 8, August 19, 1851, p. 401)

Some **institutions** – most institutions, indeed – have had a **divine** origin. But most that we see prevailing in society nothing but the form, **the shell,** is left; the life is **extinct,** and there is nothing divine in them.

(Journal II, vol. 8, August 19, 1851, pp. 403-404)

SECTION II
Spirituality & Nature

The morning **wind** forever blows, the poem of creation is **uninterrupted**; but **few are** the ears that hear it.

(*Walden*, "Where I Lived," p. 94)

Every **morning** was a cheerful invitation to make **my life of equal simplicity, and I may say innocence,** with Nature herself ... I got up early **and bathed in the pond; that was a religious exercise, and one of** the best things which I did.

(*Walden*, "Where I Lived," p. 98)

That man who does not believe that each day contains an earlier, more sacred, and auroral hour than he has yet profaned, has despaired of life, and is pursuing a descending and darkening way.

(*Walden*, "Where I've Lived," p. 99)

The millions are awake enough for physical labor: but only **one** in a million is awake enough for effective intellectual exertion, only **one in a** hundred million **to a** poetic or divine life.

(*Walden*, "Where I've Lived," p. 100)

To be awake is to be alive. I have never met **a man** who was **quite awake.**

(*Walden*, "Where I've Lived," p. 100)

I went to the **woods** because I wished to live deliberately, to front only the essential fact of life, and see if I could not learn what it had to teach, and not, when I came to die, discovered that I had not lived.

(*Walden*, "Where I've Lived," pp. 100-101)

I wanted to **live deep** and **suck** out all the **marrow of life.**

(*Walden*, "Where I've Lived," p. 101)

Our life is fritted away by detail ...
Simplify, simplify!

(*Walden*, "Where I've Lived," pp. 101-102)

Why should **we live** with such **hurry** and **waste** of life? We are determined to be **starved** before **we are hungry.**

(*Walden*, "Where I've Lived," p. 103)

Every man **is tasked** to make his life, *even in* its details, worthy of **contemplation** of his most elevated and **critical** hour.

(*Walden*, "Where I've Lived," p. 100)

In eternity there is indeed something true and sublime. But all **these times and places** and occasions are now and here. God Himself **culminates** in the **present moment,** and will never be more divine **in the lapse** of all the ages.

(*Walden*, "Where I've Lived," p. 107)

Time is but a stream I go a-fishing in. I drink at it; but while I drink I see the sandy bottom and detect how shallow it is. Its thin current slides away, but eternity remains.

(*Walden*, "Where I've Lived," p. 109)

A written word is the choicest of relics.

(*Walden*, "Reading," p. 114)

Sometimes, in a **summer morning,** having taken my accustomed bath, I sat in my **sunny doorway** from sunrise 'til noon, rapt in a reverie, amidst the pines and hickories and sumachs, in **undisturbed solitude and stillness,** while the **birds sang** around or flitted noiseless through the house, until by the sun falling in at my west window, or the noise of some traveler's wagon on the distant highway, I was reminded of the lapse of time.

(*Walden*, "Sounds," pp. 123-124)

... kill time

without injuring
eternity.

(Walden, "Economy," p. 8)

Follow your genius closely enough, and it will not fail **to show you a fresh** prospect every **hour**.

(*Walden*, "Sounds," p. 125)

Every path **but your own** is the **path of fate.** Keep on your own track, then.

(Walden, "Sounds," p. 131)

This is a **delicious evening,** when the whole body is **one sense,** and **imbibes** delight through every pore. **I go and come with a strange liberty in Nature,** a part of herself.

(*Walden*, "Solitude," p. 143)

I find it wholesome to be alone the greater part of the time. To be in company, even with the best, is soon wearisome and dissipating. I love to be alone. I never found the companion that was so companionable as solitude … Solitude is not measured by the miles of space that intervene between a man and his fellows.

(*Walden*, "Solitude," p. 150)

I have a great deal of company in my house; especially in the morning, when nobody calls.

(*Walden*, "Solitude," p. 151)

Shall I not have intelligence with the earth? Am I not partly leaves and vegetable **myself?**

(*Walden*, "Solitude," p. 153)

Shall I not have intelligence with the earth? Am I not partly leaves and vegetable myself?

(*Walden*, "Solitude," p. 153)

I have a great deal of company in my house; especially in the morning, when nobody calls.

(*Walden*, "Solitude," p. 151)

A lake is the landscape's most beautiful and **expressive** feature. **It is the earth's eye;** looking into which the beholder measures the depth of his own nature.

(*Walden*, "The Ponds," pp. 206-207)

Nothing so fair, so pure, and at the **same time** so large, **as a lake,** perchance, lies on **the surface** of the earth. **Sky water.**

(*Walden*, "The Ponds," p. 209)

Nature has **no human inhabitant** who appreciates her ... **Talk of heaven! Ye disgrace earth!**

(*Walden*, "The Ponds," p. 222)

Rise from care beyond the dawn, and seek adventures.

(*Walden*, "Baker Farm," p. 230)

Enjoy the land, but own it not.

(*Walden*, "Baker Farm," p. 230)

As I came home through the woods with my string of fish, trailing my pole, it being quite dark, I caught a glimpse of a woodchuck stealing across my path, and felt a strange thrill of savage delight, and was strongly tempted to seize and devour him raw; not that I was hungry then, except for what wilderness which he represented.

(*Walden*, "Higher Laws," p. 232)

No humane being past the thoughtless age of **boyhood,** will wantonly murder any **creature** which holds its life by the same **tenure** that he does ... Thus, even in civilized communities, the embryo man passed through the **hunter stage** of development.

(*Walden*, "Higher Laws," p. 235)

If the day and night are such that you greet them **with joy,** and life emits a **fragrance** like flowers and sweet-scented herbs, is more elastic, **more starry,** more **immortal** – that is your success.

(*Walden*, "Higher Laws," p. 239)

I believe that **water** is the only drink for a **wise** man ...

(*Walden*, "Higher Laws," p. 240)

No man ever followed his genius till it misled him.

(*Walden,* "Higher Laws," p. 239)

There is never **an instant's** truce between virtue and vice. **Goodness is the** only **investment** that never fails.

(*Walden*, "Higher Laws," p. 241)

He who **distinguishes** the true savor of his food can never be a **glutton;** he who does not **cannot be otherwise.**

(*Walden*, "Higher Laws," p. 241)

Chastity is the flowering of man; and what are called Genius, Heroism, Holiness, and the like, are but **various fruits** which succeed it. Man flows at once to God when the **channel of purity** is opened ... He is blessed who is asserted that the animal is dying out in him day **by day, and the divine being established.**

(*Walden*, "Higher Laws," p. 243)

You only need sit still long enough in some attractive **spot in the woods** that all its **inhabitants** may exhibit themselves to you …

(*Walden*, "Brute Neighbors," p. 253)

Heaven is
under our feet as well as over our **heads.**

(*Walden*, "The Pond in Winter," p. 313)

The **particular** laws are **our** points of view, as, to the **traveler,** a mountain outline varies with **every step,** and it has an infinite number of profiles, **through absolutely but one form.**

(*Walden*, "The Pond in Winter," p. 320)

The **day** is an epitome of the year. The night is the **winter,** the morning and evening are the spring and fall, **and the noon is the summer.**

(*Walden*, "Spring," p. 332)

In a pleasant spring morning all men's sins are forgiven.

(*Walden*, "Spring," p. 346)

At the same time that we are **earnest** to explore and learn all things, we require that all things be mysterious and **unexplorable,** that land and sea be infinitely wild, unsurveyed, and unfathomed by us. We can never have **enough** of Nature.

(*Walden*, "Spring," p. 350)

My profession is to be always **on the alert to find God in nature, to know** his lerking-places, **to attend all** oratorios, the **opera,** in nature.

(Journal II, vol. 8, September 7, 1851, p. 470)

I learned this, at least, by my **experiment:** that if one **advances** confidently in the direction of **his dreams,** and endeavors to live the life which he has **imagined,** he will meet with **a success unexpected** in **common** hours.

(*Walden*, "Conclusion," p. 356)

In proportion as he simplifies his life, the laws of the universe will appear less complex ...

(*Walden*, "Conclusion," p. 356)

If you have **built castles** in the air, your work need not be lost; that is where they should be. Now put the **foundations under them.**

(*Walden*, "Conclusion," p. 356)

I desire to speak somewhere without bounds; like a man in a **waking moment, to men** in their waking moments; for I am convinced that **I cannot exaggerate enough even** to lay the foundation of **true** expression.

(*Walden*, "Conclusion," p. 357)

However mean your life is, meet it and live it; **do not shun it** or call it hard names. It is not so bad as you are. It looks **poorest** when you are richest. The fault-finder will find faults even **in paradise.** Love your life, **poor as it is.**

(*Walden*, "Conclusion," p. 361)

Cultivate poverty like a garden herb, like sage. Do not trouble yourself much to get new things, whether cloths or friends ... Things do not change: we change. Sell your clothes and keep your thoughts.

(*Walden*, "Conclusion," p. 361)

Rather than love, than money, than fame, **give me** truth.

(*Walden*, "Conclusion," p. 360)

Only that day dawns to which we are awake. There is more day to dawn. The sun is but a morning star.

(*Walden*, "Conclusion," p. 367)

I perceive that, when **an acorn and a chestnut** fall side by side, the one does not remain inert to make way for the other, but both obey their own laws, **and spring** and grow and **flourish** as best they can, till one, perchance, overshadows and **destroys** the other. **If a plant** cannot live according to its nature, it dies; and so a man.

(*Civil Disobedience*, p. 376)

Truth is always in harmony with herself, and it is **not concerned** chiefly to reveal the justice that may **consist** with wrong-doing.

(*Civil Disobedience*, p. 384)

We should go forth on the **shortest walk,** perchance, in the spirit of **undying adventure,** never to return – prepared **to send back our embalmed** hearts **only as** relics to our desolate kingdoms. If you are ready to leave father, mother, and brother and sister, and wife and child and friends, and **never see them again** – if you have paid your debts, and made your will, and settled all your affairs, and are **a free man,** then you are ready for a walk.

(*Walking*, p. 206)

No wealth can buy the requisite leisure, freedom, and independence, which are the capital in this profession. It comes only by the grace of God. It requires a direct dispensation from Heaven to become a walker. You must be born into the family of the Walkers.

(*Walking*, p. 207)

I think that I cannot **preserve my health and spirits,** unless **I spend** four hours a day at least – and it is **commonly more** than that – **sauntering** through the woods and over the hills and fields, **absolutely free** from all **worldly engagements.**

(*Walking*, p. 207)

Even sects of **philosophers** have felt the necessity of importing the woods to themselves, **since they did not go to the woods.**

(*Walking*, p. 211)

... **go** in search of the springs **of life.**

(*Walking*, p. 209)

I believe that there is a subtle magnetism in Nature, which, if we unconsciously yield to it, will **direct** us aright.

(*Walking*, p. 216)

The fact is I am a **mystic,** a **transcendentalist,** and a natural philosopher to boot.

(Journal V, vol. II, March 5, 1853, p. 4)

Dwell as near as possible to the channel in which your life **flows.**

(Journal V, vol. II, March 12, 1853, p. 17)

I have an **appointment** with spring. She comes to **the window** to wake me, and **I go forth** an hour or two earlier than usual.

(Journal V, vol. II, March 22, 1853, p. 36)

To stay in the house all day, such reviving spring days as the past have been, bending over a stove and gnawing one's heart, seems to me as absurd as for a woodchuck to linger in his burrow.

(Journal V, vol. II, March 22, 1853, p. 37)

... not till we are lost
do we begin to realize
where we are ...

(Journal V, vol. II, March 29, 1853, p. 64)

If I am **overflowing** with life, am rich in **experience** for which I lack **expression,** then nature will be my language …

(Journal V, vol. II, May 10, 1853, p. 135)

... not till we are lost
do we begin to realize
where we are ...

(Journal V, vol. II, March 29, 1853, p. 64)

Section II: Spirituality & Nature

If I am **overflowing** with life, am rich in **experience** for which I lack **expression,** then nature will be my language ...

(Journal V, vol. II, May 10, 1853, p. 135)

We bathe thus first in air; then, when the air has warmed it, in water.

(Journal V, vol. II, May 15, 1853, p. 159)

Ah, the beauty of this last hour of the day – when a **power** stills the air and smooth[e]s **all waters** and all minds – that partakes of the light of the day and the **stillness** of the **night!**

(Journal V, vol. II, May 17, 1853, p. 167)

Nature is beautiful only as a place where a life is **to be lived.** It is not beautiful to him who has **not resolved** on a beautiful life.

(Journal V, vol. II, July 20, 1853, p. 323)

The year is full of warnings of its **shortness,** as is **life.**

(Journal V, vol. II, August 18, 1853, p. 379)

For all of Nature is doing her best each moment **to make us well. She exists** for **no other end.** Do not **resist** her.

(Journal V, vol. II, August 23, 1853, p. 395)

What if God were to **confide** in us for a moment! Should we **not** then be **gods?**

(*Familiar Letters and Index vol. 6*, "Letter to Ralph Waldo Emerson," February 12, 1843, p. 56)

The present hour is always wealthiest when it is **poorer** than the future ones ...

(*Familiar Letters and Index vol. 6*,
"Letter to Richard Fuller,"
April 2, 1843, p. 66)

To set about living a truer life is to go [on] a journey to a distant country, gradually to find ourselves surrounded by new scenes and men; and as long as the old are around me, I know I am not in any true sense living a newer or better life.

(*Familiar Letters and Index vol.* 6, "Letter to Harrison Blake," March 27, 1848, p. 160)

I do not believe that **the outward** and the **inward life** correspond; that if any should succeed to live a **higher life,** others would not know of it; that difference and **distance** are one ... The outward is **only** the outside of that which is **within.**

(*Familiar Letters and Index vol. 6*, "Letter to Harrison Blake," March 27, 1848, p. 160)

... simplify the problem of life, distinguish the **necessary** and the real. Probe the earth to see where your main **roots** run.

(*Familiar Letters and Index* vol. 6, "Letter to Harrison Blake," March 27, 1848, p. 161)

If a man constantly aspires, is he not elevated?

(*Familiar Letters and Index vol. 6,*
"Letter to Harrison Blake,"
March 27, 1848, p. 162)

Every man's position is in fact too simple to be described. I have sworn no oath. I have no designs on society, Nature, or God. I am simply what I am, or I begin to be that. I live in the present. I only remember the past, and anticipate the future. I love to live.

(*Familiar Letters and Index vol. 6*, "Letter to Harrison Blake," March 27, 1848, p. 162)

Men will believe what they see.
Let him see.

(*Familiar Letters and Index vol. 6*, "Letter to Harrison Blake," March 27, 1848, p. 163)

**Be not simply good;
be good for something.**

(*Familiar Letters and Index vol. 6*,
"Letter to Harrison Blake,"
March 27, 1848, p. 164)

Let nothing come between you and the light ... When you **travel** to the Celestial City, carry **no letter** of introduction. When you knock, ask to see God – **none** of the servants.

(*Familiar Letters and Index vol. 6*, "Letter to Harrison Blake," March 27, 1848, p. 164)

What Nature is to the mind she is also **to the body.** As she feeds my *imagination,* she will **feed my body ...**

(*Familiar Letters and Index* vol. 6, "Letter to Harrison Blake," March 27, 1848, p. 166)

There is not necessarily any **gross** and ugly **fact** which may not be eradicated from the life of man. We should **endeavor** practically in our lives to correct all the defects which our **imagination** detects. The heavens are as deep as our imaginations are **high.**

(*Familiar Letters and Index vol. 6*, "Letter to Harrison Blake," March 27, 1848, p. 166)

But whatever we do we must do **confidently** ... **not expecting more light, but having** light enough.

(*Familiar Letters and Index* vol. 6, "Letter to Harrison Blake," March 27, 1848, pp. 166-167)

All transcendent goodness is one, though **appreciated** in different ways, or by different **senses.**

(*Familiar Letters and Index vol. 6,* "Letter to Harrison Blake," September 1852, p. 198)

Life is so short that it is not wise to take roundabout ways, nor can we spend much time in waiting.

(*Familiar Letters and Index vol. 6*, "Letter to Harrison Blake," September 1852, p. 220)

The day is never so dark, nor the night even, but that **the laws** at least of light still **prevail,** and so may make it light in our minds if they are **open to the truth.**

(*Familiar Letters and Index vol. 6*, "Letter to Harrison Blake," December 19, 1854, p. 242)

Section II: Spirituality & Nature

Is the air sweet to you? Do you find anything at **which you can work, accomplishing** something solid from day to day?

(*Familiar Letters and Index vol. 6*, "Letter to Harrison Blake," September 26, 1855, p. 260)

It is surprising how contented one can be with nothing definite – only a **sense** of existence.

(*Familiar Letters and Index vol. 6*, "Letter to Harrison Blake," 1853, p. 294)

I should not like to exchange any of my life for money.

(*Familiar Letters and Index vol. 6*,
"Letter to Harrison Blake,"
December 31, 1856, p. 303)

You must have been **enriched** by your solitary **walk** over the mountains. **I suppose that I feel that same awe** when on their summits that many do on **entering** a church.

(*Familiar Letters and Index vol. 6*, "Letter to Harrison Blake," November 16, 1857, p. 319)

What did the mountain say? What did the **mountain** do? **I keep** a mountain anchored off eastward a little way, which I ascend in my dreams both **awake** and asleep.

(*Familiar Letters and Index vol. 6*, "Letter to Harrison Blake," November 16, 1857, p. 321)

No thinker can afford to overlook the influence of the **moon** any **more than the astronomer** can.

(Journal III, vol. 9, September 21, 1851, p. 8)

The fairies are a **quiet, gentle folk,** invented plainly to inhabit the **moonlight** … As moonlight is to **sunlight,** so are the fairies **to men.**

(Journal III, vol. 9, October 5, 1851, p. 47)

It is a bright, clear, **warm** November day. I feel blessed. I love my life. I am **warm** toward all nature.

(Journal III, vol. 9, November 1, 1851, p. 86)

...at **sundown** I hear the hooting of an owl ... I rejoice that there are **owls**. They represent the **stark, twilight,** unsatisfied thoughts I have ... This sound **faintly** suggests the infinite **roominess** of nature, that there is a world in which owls **live.**

(Journal III, vol. 9, November 16, 1851, pp. 122-123)

Ah, dear nature, the mere remembrance, after a short forgetfulness, of the pine woods! I come to it as a hungry man to a crust of bread.

(Journal III, vol. 9, December 12, 1851, p. 133)

I wished to dive into some **deep stream** of thoughtful and **devoted** life, which meandered through **retired and fertile meadows far from towns.** I wished to do it again, or for once, things quite congenial to my **highest** inmost and most sacred **nature,** to lurk in crystalline thought like the trout under **verdurous** banks, **where stray mankind should only see my bubble** come to the surface. I wished to live, **ah!** As far away **as man can think.**

(Journal III, vol. 9, December 12, 1851, p. 133)

The pines looked like old friends again.

(Journal III, vol. 9, December 13, 1851, p. 136)

Ah, give me pure mind, pure thought! Let me not be in haste to detect the universal law; let me see more clearly a particular instance of it!

(Journal III, vol. 9, December 25, 1851, p. 157)

... you may **build yourself up** to the highest of your conceptions, that you may remember your Creator in the days of your **youth** and justify his ways to man, that the end of your life may not be its amusement, speak – though your thought **presupposes** the non-existence of your hearers – thoughts that transcend life and **death.** What thought mortal ears are not fitted to hear absolute truth!

(Journal III, vol. 9, December 25, 1851, p. 157-158)

We look upward for inspiration ...
The sky is always ready to answer to our moods ...

(Journal III, vol. 9, December 25 & 27, 1851, pp. 158-159)

The man is blessed who every day is permitted to behold anything so pure and serene as the western sky at sunset ...

(Journal III, vol. 9, December 27, 1851, p. 159)

Yesterday **nobody** dreamed of **today**; **nobody** dreams of **tomorrow.**

(Journal III, vol. 9, December 29, 1851, p. 161)

Let me **not live** as if time was short. Catch the pace of the seasons ... Let your life be a leisurely progress through the **realms** of nature, even in guest-quarters.

(Journal III, vol. 9, January 11, 1852, p. 182)

I sometimes think that I may **go forth** and walk hard and **earnestly,** and live a **more substantial** life and get a **glorious** experience ... But then **swiftly** the thought comes to me, [g]o not so far out of your way for a truer life; keep **strictly** onward in **that path** alone which your **genius** points out.

(Journal III, vol. 9, January 12, 1852, p. 184)

Live a purer, a more thoughtful and laborious life, more **true** to your friends and neighbors, **more noble** and magnanimous ... To live in **relations** of truth and sincerity with men is to dwell in a **frontier** country.

(Journal III, vol. 9, January 12, 1852, pp. 184-185)

Men talk about traveling this way or that, as if seeing were all in the **eyes,** and a man could **sufficiently** report what he stood bodily before, when the **seeing** depends ever on the **being.**

(Journal III, vol. 9, January 12, 1852, p. 185)

... that which is farthest off is the symbol of what is deepest within. The lover of contemplation, accordingly, will gaze much into the sky ... As the skies appear to a man, so is his mind.

(Journal III, vol. 9, January 17, 1852, p. 201)

Section II: Spirituality & Nature

My **thoughts** are my company. They have a certain **individuality** and separate **existence, aye, personality.**

(Journal III, vol. 9, January 22, 1852, p. 217)

For I was **rich,** if not in money, in sunny hours and **summer days,** and **spent them lavishly.**

(Journal III, vol. 9, January 25, 1852, p. 229)

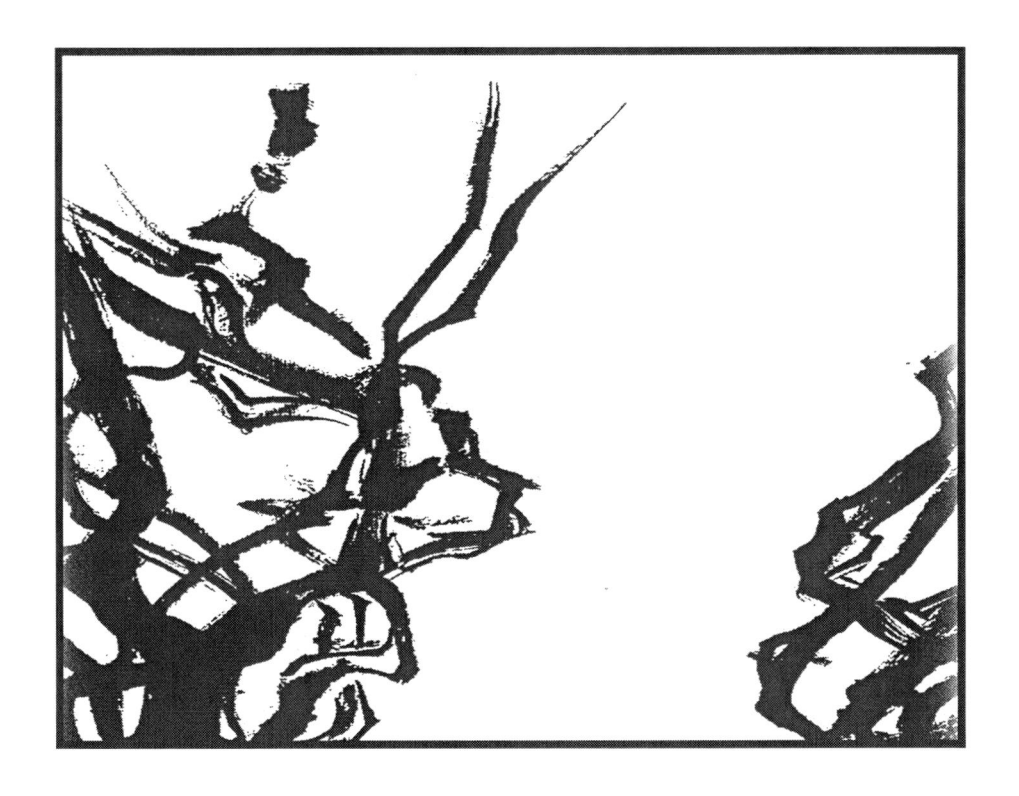

Poetry implies the whole truth. Philosophy expresses a **particle** of it ... Let all things give way to the **impulse** of expression.

(Journal III, vol. 9, January 26, 1852, p. 232)

Our life should be so active and progressive as to be a journey.

(Journal III, vol. 9, January 28, 1852, p. 240)

A wakeful **night** will yield as much thought as a **long** journey.

(Journal III, vol. 9, January 30, 1852, p. 255)

Each thing
is attached to each, and running to coalesce like drops of water.

(Journal III, vol. 9, February 1, 1852, p. 265)

I suspect that the child plucks its first flower with an insight into its beauty and significance which the subsequent botanist never retains.

(Journal III, vol. 9, February 4, 1852, p. 279)

...take wider views of the universe.

(Journal III, vol. 9, April 2, 1852, p. 381)

Dreams are real, as in the light of the stars and **moon**, and theirs is said to be **a dreamy light.** Such **early morning** thoughts as I speak of occupy **a debatable** ground between dreams and **waking thoughts.** They are a sort of **permanent** dream in my mind.

(Journal X, vol. 16, October 29, 1857, p. 141)

The love of Nature and fullest perception of the **revelation** which she is to man is not compatible with **the belief** in [a] peculiar revelation [in] **the Bible** ...

(Journal X, vol. 16, October 29, 1857, p. 147)

It is only a reflecting mind that sees reflections.

(Journal X, vol. 16, November 2, 1857, pp. 156-157)

Sympathy with nature is an evidence of perfect health.

(Journal X, vol. 16, November 18, 1857, p. 188)

You cannot perceive **beauty** but with a **serene** mind.

(Journal X, vol. 16, November 18, 1857, p. 188)

You feel the fertilizing influence of the rain in your mind. **The part** of **you that is** wettest is **fullest** of life ... **You discover evidences** of immortality **not known** to divines. You cease **to die.** You detect some **sprouts** of life. Every step in the old rye-field is on **virgin** soil.

(Journal X, vol. 16, January 26, 1857, p. 262)

Walking by the river this afternoon … I inhale a fresh, meadowy, spring odor … which is a little exciting. It is like the fragrance of tea to an old tea-drinker.

(Journal X, vol. 16, March 16, 1858, p. 296)

Truth strikes us from behind, and in the dark, as well as from before and in broad **daylight.**

(Journal I, vol. 7, November 5, 1837, p. 8)

Truth is ever returning into herself. I glimpse one feature today, **another** tomorrow; and the **next day** they are blended.

(Journal I, vol. 7, November 13, 1837, p. 9)

If there is **nothing new on earth**, still **there is** something new in the heavens. We have always a resource in **the skies.** They are **constantly** turning a new page to view. The wind sets the types in this blue ground, and the inquiring may always read a new truth.

(Journal I, vol. 7, November 13, 1837, p. 11)

No faculty in man was created with a useless or sinister intent; in **no respect** can he be **wholly bad** ...

(Journal I, vol. 7, December 12, 1837, p. 16)

In the **last stage** of civilization Poetry, Religion and Philosophy will be **one** ...

(Journal I, vol. 7, December 17, 1837, p. 18)

Section II: Spirituality & Nature

... the life of every man is a profound secret.

(Journal I, vol. 7, March 14, 1838, p. 36)

Silence is the communing of a conscious soul with itself. If the **soul** attends for a moment to its own infinity, then and there is silence. She is audible to all **men,** at all times, in all places, and if we will we may always hearken to her **admonitions.**

(Journal I, vol. 7, December 15, 1838, p. 64)

To the **sensitive soul**, the universe has its own fixed measure, which is its measure also, and, as a regular pulse is **inseparable** from a **healthy body**, so is its healthiness dependent on the regularity of its rhythm. In all sounds the soul recognizes its own **rhythm** … When the body **marches** to the measure of the soul, then [there] is true **courage** and invincible strength.

(Journal I, vol. 7, December 1839, pp. 103-104)

We are one **virtue,**
one truth,
one **beauty.**

(Journal I, vol. 7, December 1839, p. 107)

Truth has properly no opponent, for nothing gets so far up on the other side as to be opposite. She looks broadcast over the field and sees no opponent.

(Journal I, vol. 7, February 11, 1840, p. 118)

Beauty
lives by
rhythms.

(Journal I, vol. 7, February 14, 1840, p. 119)

An early morning walk is a blessing for the whole day.

(Journal I, vol. 7, April 20, 1840, p. 134)

Perfect sincerity and **transparency** make a great part of beauty, as in **dewdrops,** lakes, and **diamonds.**

(Journal I, vol. 7, June 20, 1840, p. 145)

If we only see clearly enough how mean our lives are, they will be splendid enough. Let us remember not to strive upwards too long, but sometimes drop plumb down the other way, and wallow in meanness. From the deepest pit we may see the stars, if not the sun. Let us have presence of mind enough to sink when we can't swim.

(Journal I, vol. 7, June 20, 1840, p. 146)

Our life is but the Soul made known by its fruits, the body ... **Make yourself** a **perfect** body.

(Journal I, vol. 7, June 21, 1840, p. 147)

Truth
is always paradoxical.

(Journal I, vol. 7, June 26, 1840, p. 153)

Great thoughts
make
great **men.**

(Journal I, vol. 7, February 7, 1841, p. 204)

Words do not lose their **truth** by time or misinterpretation, but stand **unscathed longer** than he who **spoke** them.

(Journal I, vol. 7, February 10, 1841, p. 210)

There is **elevation** in every hour. No part of the earth is so low and **withdrawn** that the heavens cannot be seen from it, but every part supports the sky.

(Journal I, vol. 7, February 15, 1841, p. 214)

In the love of narrow souls I make many short voyages, but in vain; I find no sea room. But in great souls I sail before the wind without a watch, and never reach the shore.

(Journal I, vol. 7, February 19, 1841, p. 218)

It is **always**
a short **step** to
peace of mind.

(Journal I, vol. 7, March 27, 1841, p. 241)

The **gods** are of no sect; they side with **no man.**

(Journal I, vol. 7, April 15, 1841, p. 249)

The **fickle** person is he that does not know what is true or right **absolutely** – who has not an ancient wisdom for a lifetime, but a new **prudence** for every **hour.**

(Journal I, vol. 7, May 6, 1841, p. 257)

If I am not I, who will be?

(Journal I, vol. 7, August 9, 1841, p. 270)

Let us know and conform only to the fashions of **eternity.**

(Journal I, vol. 7, September 1, 1841, p. 278)

Heaven is the **inmost place. **The **good** have not to travel **far.**

(Journal I, vol. 7, December 29, 1841, p. 301)

Virtue is the **deed** of the bravest. It is that art which demands the **greatest** confidence and fearlessness. Only some hardy soul **ventures** upon it.

(Journal I, vol. 7, January 1, 1842, p. 308)

The ringing of the church bell is a much more melodious sound than any that is heard within the church.

(Journal I, vol. 7, January 2, 1842, p. 309)

There must be some **narrowness** in the **soul** that compels one to have **secrets.**

(Journal I, vol. 7, February 21, 1842, p. 322)

Consider what a difference there is between living and dying. **To die is not to begin to die, and continue;** it is not a **state** of continuance, but of **transientness;** but to live is a condition of continuance, and does not mean to be born merely. There is no continuance of death. It is a transient phenomenon. **Nature** presents **nothing** in a state of death.

(Journal I, vol. 7, March 12, 1842, pp. 327-328)

Life is grand, and so are its environments of Past and Future. Would the **face** of nature be so serene and beautiful if man's destiny were not **equally** so?

(Journal I, vol. 7, March 14, 1842, p. 330)

It is a new day; the sun shines.

(Journal I, vol. 7, March 15, 1842, p. 330)

Life is grand, and so are its environments of Past and Future. Would the **face** of nature be so serene and beautiful if man's destiny were not **equally** so?

(Journal I, vol. 7, March 14, 1842, p. 330)

It is a new **day;**
the sun shines.

(Journal I, vol. 7, March 15, 1842, p. 330)

What is all **nature** and human life at this moment, what the **scenery** and **vicinity** of a human soul, but the **song** of an early sparrow ...

(Journal I, vol. 7, March 20, 1842, p. 341)

A man's life should be as fresh as a river. It should be the same channel, but a new water every instant.

(Journal I, vol. 7, March 25, 1842, p. 347)

The stars are
God's dreams,
thoughts remembered in the
silence of his night.

(Journal I, vol. 7, March 25, 1842, p. 349)

All sights and sounds are seen and heard both in time and eternity. And when the eternity of any sight or sound strikes the eye or ear, [we] are intoxicated with delight.

(Journal I, vol. 7, April 3, 1842, p. 359)

The Great Spirit makes **indifferent** all times and places. The place where he is seen is always the same, and indescribably **pleasant** to all our **senses.**

(Journal I, vol. 7, July 7, 1845, p. 363)

Section II: Spirituality & Nature / 245

Behold these flowers! Let us be up with Time, not **dreaming** of three thousand years ago ... Where is the spirit of **that time** but in this **present** day ... Three thousand years ago are not agone; they are still lingering here this **summer** morn[ing].

(Journal I, vol. 7, August 6, 1845, p. 376)

All nature is ...
akin to art.

(Journal I, vol. 7, August 1845, p. 380)

Of what **significance** the light of day, if it is not the reflection of an **inward** dawn? – to what **purpose** is the veil of night withdrawn, if the morning reveals **nothing** to the soul?

(*Excursions and Poems*, "Night and Moonlight," p. 332)

Man flows at once to God as soon as the channel of purity, physical, **intellectual** and **moral,** is open.

(Journal II, vol. 8, 1850, p. 4)

It is **wisest** to live without any definite and recognized **object** from day to day – any particular object – for the world is **round,** and we are not to live on **a tangent** or a radius to the **sphere.**

(Journal II, vol. 8, 1850, p. 8)

There is a
time for
everything.

(Journal II, vol. 8, 1850, p. 16)

Men talk about miracles in the Bible because there is no **miracle** in their lives.

(Journal II, vol. 8, June 1850, p. 33)

Our thoughts are the epochs of our life: all else is but as a **journal** of the winds that blew while we were here.

(Journal II, vol. 8, 1850, p. 43)

All the past is equally a failure and a success; it is a success in as much as it offers you the present opportunity.

(Journal II, vol. 8, 1850, p. 44)

As to **conforming** outwardly, and living your **live** inwardly, I have **not a very** high **opinion** of that ...

(Journal II, vol. 8, 1850, p. 48)

It is **important** to **observe** not only the subject of our **pure** and unalloyed joys, but also the secret of any **dissatisfaction** one may **feel.**

(Journal II, vol. 8, February 13, 1851, p. 159)

Imagine yourself alone in the world, a musing, **wondering** reflecting spirit, lost in **thought,** and imagine **thereafter** the creation of man! – man made in the **image** of **God!**

(Journal II, vol. 8, May 21, 1851, p. 208)

You may walk out in any **direction** over the earth's surface, lifting your horizon, and everywhere your path, **climbing** the convexity of the **globe,** leads you between heaven and earth, not away from **the light of the sun and the stars** and the habitations of men.

(Journal II, vol. 8, June 7, 1851, p. 228)

My most sacred and memorable life is commonly on awaking in the morning. I frequently awake with an **atmosphere** about me as if my **unremembered** dreams had been divine, as if my spirit had journeyed to its native **place,** and, in the act of **reentering** its native body, had diffused a … fragrance around. The Genius says: "Ah! That is what you were! That is what you may yet be!" It is **glorious** for us to be able to regret even such an existence.

(Journal II, vol. 8, May 24, 1851, p. 213)

We do not **commonly** live our life out and full; we do not fill **our pores** with our blood; we do not **inspire** fully and entirely enough ... We live but a *fraction* of our life.

(Journal II, vol. 8, June 13, 1851, p. 251)

My pulse must beat with Nature.

(Journal II, vol. 8, June 22, 1851, p. 268)

... by simply **living,** by honesty of purpose. We live and **rejoice.**

(Journal II, vol. 8, June 22, 1851, p. 268)

Let me forever go in search of myself; never for a **moment** think that I have **found** myself; be as stranger to myself, never a familiar, seeking **acquaintance** still.

(Journal II, vol. 8, July 16, 1851, pp. 314-315)

... I have **freedom** in my thought[s], and in **my** soul [I] am **free.**

(Journal II, vol. 8, July 21, 1851, p. 325)

Sing while you may, before evil days come. He that ha[s] ears, let him hear. **See, hear, smell, taste,** etc., while these senses are fresh and pure. There is always a kind of Aeolian harp music to be heard in the air ... The occupied ear thinks that beyond the cricket **no sound can be heard, but there is an immortal melody** that may be heard in the morning, noon, and night, **by ears that can attend, and from time to time this man or that hears it,** having ears that were made for music.

(Journal II, vol. 8, July 21, 1851, p. 330)

Section II: Spirituality & Nature

...what **infinite** faith and **promise** and **moderation** begins [with] each new day!

(Journal II, vol. 8, August 12, 1851, p. 384)

The man must not drink [from] the running streams, **the living waters,** who is not **prepared** to have all nature reborn in him ...

(Journal II, vol. 8, August 17, 1851, p. 393)

All perception of **truth** is the detection of an **analogy;** we reason from our **hands** to our head.

(Journal II, vol. 8, September 5, 1851, p. 463)

Our moments of **inspiration** are not lost though we have no particular poem to **show** for them; for those **experiences** have left an indelible **impression,** and we are ever and anon reminded of them.

(Journal II, vol. 8, September 7, 1851, p. 469)

The scenery, when it is truly seen, reacts on the life of the seer. How to live. How to get the most life … How to extract its honey from the flower of the world. That is my everyday business. I am busy as a bee about it.

(Journal II, vol. 8, September 7, 1851, p. 470)

SECTION III
Love

To be married at least should be the one poetical act of a man's life.

(Journal V, vol. II, August 11, 1853, p. 369)

What the essential **difference** between **man and woman** is, that they **should** be thus attracted to one another, no one has satisfactorily **answered.**

(*Familiar Letters and Index* vol. 6, "Letter to Harrison Blake," September 1852, p. 198)

Man is **continually** saying to woman, Why will you not be **more wise?** Woman is continually saying to man, **Why will you not** be more loving? It is **not in their** wills to be wise or to be loving; but, unless **each is both** wise and loving, there can be **neither** wisdom or **love.**

(*Familiar Letters and Index* vol. 6, "Letter to Harrison Blake," September 1852, p. 198)

The **lover** sees in the glance of his beloved the same beauty that in the **sunset** paints the **western** skies.

(*Familiar Letters and Index vol. 6*, "Letter to Harrison Blake," September 1852, p. 198)

One may be **drunk** with love without being any **nearer** to finding his **mate.**

(*Familiar Letters and Index vol. 6*, "Letter to Harrison Blake," September 1852, p. 198)

Love is a severe critic.

(*Familiar Letters and Index vol. 6*, "Letter to Harrison Blake," September 1852, p. 200)

Love must be as much as a light as a flame.

(*Familiar Letters and Index vol. 6*,
"Letter to Harrison Blake,"
September 1852, p. 200)

The **heart** is blind;
but love is **not** blind.

(*Familiar Letters and Index vol. 6*,
"Letter to Harrison Blake,"
September 1852, p. 200)

In love and friendship the imagination is as much exercised as the heart; and if either is outraged the other will be estranged.

(*Familiar Letters and Index vol.* 6, "Letter to Harrison Blake," September 1852, p. 200)

Love is the profoundest of secrets.

(Familiar Letters and Index vol. 6, "Letter to Harrison Blake," September 1852, p. 201)

All lusts or base pleasures **must give place** to **loftier** delights.

(*Familiar Letters and Index vol. 6*, "Letter to Harrison Blake," September 1852, p. 205)

Love and lust are far asunder.

(*Familiar Letters and Index vol. 6,*
"Letter to Harrison Blake,"
September 1852, p. 206)

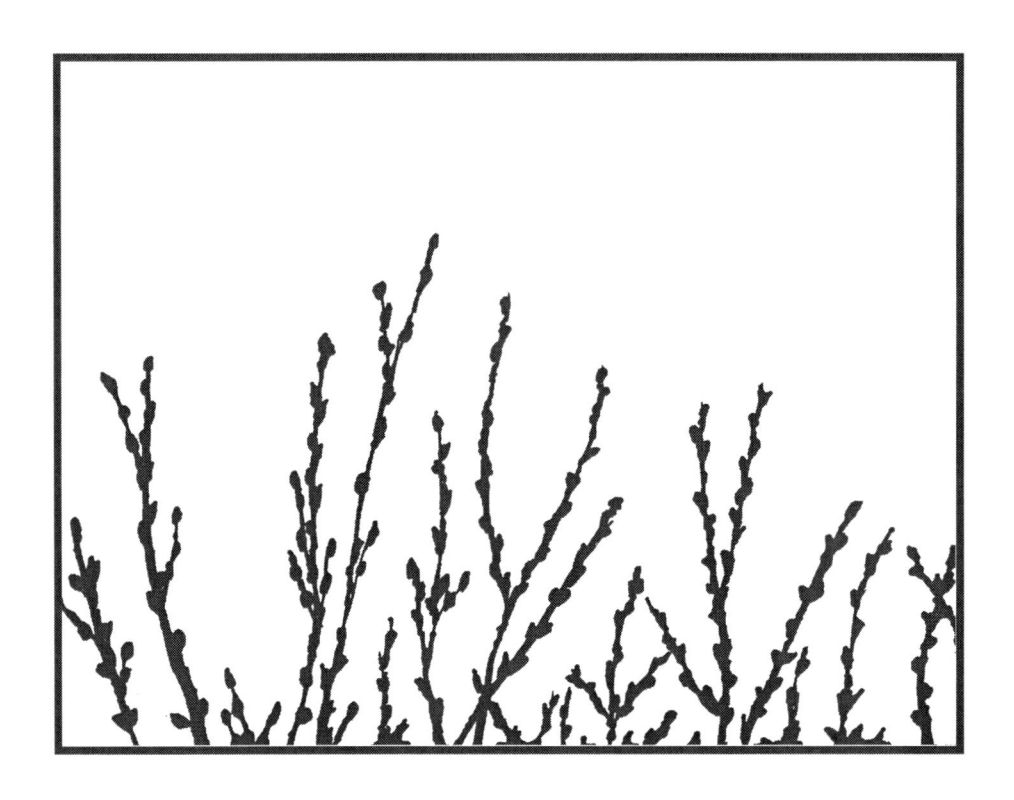

Love and lust are as **far asunder** as a flower-garden is from a **brothel.**

(*Familiar Letters and Index vol. 6*, "Letter to Harrison Blake," September 1852, p. 207)

Let love be purified, and the rest will follow.

(*Familiar Letters and Index vol. 6*,
"Letter to Harrison Blake,"
September 1852, p. 208)

**Discipline yourself
only to yield to love ...**

(Journal III, vol. 9, January 30, 1852, p. 253)

The **poet's** relation
to his theme is the
relation of **lovers.**

(Journal III, vol. 9, January 30, 1852, p. 253)

All romance is grounded on friendship.

(Journal I, vol. 7, February 18, 1840, p. 121)

Love never degrades its votaries, but lifts them up to higher **walks** of beings.

(Journal I, vol. 7, March 20, 1840, p. 129)

The loftiest utterance of **Love** is, **perhaps,** sublimely satirical. Sympathy with what is sound makes **sport** of what is unsound.

(Journal I, vol. 7, June 24, 1840, p. 151)

Veneration
is the measure of
Love.

(Journal I, vol. 7, June 27, 1840, p. 154)

There is nothing so **stable** and unfluctuating as **love**.

(Journal I, vol. 7, February 21, 1841, p. 219)

Do you expect me to love with you, unless you make my **love secondary** to nothing else … ? Love that I love, and I will love thee that lovest it.

(Journal I, vol. 7, March 14, 1842, p. 329)

The only way to speak the truth is to speak lovingly; only the lover's words are heard.

(Journal I, vol. 7, March 15, 1842, p. 332)

Love is a mutual confidence whose foundations no one knows.

(Journal II, vol. 8, April 30, 1851, p. 185)

Index

A

Adventures............112
Air.......................172
America................44
Art......................247
Awake............92, 136

B

Beautiful...............153
Beauty...........109, 152
Being...................192
Believe.................163
Bible, The........20, 203
Body...................223
Books....................21

C

Character................73
Chastity................121
Children.........19, 200
Church................236
Civilization......10, 213
Clothes...................9
Communication.......12
Companion............67
Conformity............26, 233, 255
Conscience............30
Constitution, The.....42
Conceptions..........185

Contemplation.........97
Creation..................88
Critic....................277
Culture...................41

D

Day.....................240
Daylight...............209
Delight.................244
Designs................162
Desperation..............5
Destiny................239
Discipline.............286
Dissatisfaction.......256
Dreaming...............78
Dreams................129, 188, 202
Drunk..................276

E

Earth..................110, 111, 160, 211
Education..............81
Elevated...............161
Elevation..............227
Eternity..................98
Evil......................14
Existence.............173
Expression.....132, 150
Experience...........190

F

Faith..............63, 266
Fate....................104
Flowers.........116, 246
Flower-garden.......284
Freedom...............70, 82, 264
Friends...........49, 183
Friendship..............79
Food...................120
Foundations...131, 295

G

Genius................103, 118, 259
God...................128, 153, 165, 249
Government..........25, 28, 29, 31, 32, 43
Goodness............119, 164, 169
Great men............225

H

Health.................205
Heart..................279
Heaven(s)............123, 167, 234

Honesty..................262
Honey.....................270
Hungry...................96
Human...................115
Human soul...........241

I

Ignorance...................3
Inspiration......186, 269
Institutions.........85, 86
Imagination....166, 280
Imagine..................257
Intelligence............108

J

Journey...........197, 198

L

Land.......................113
Law........................35, 36, 84, 137
Leisure...................140
Life...................90, 93, 94, 143, 146, 158, 159
Light......................171
Live........................260
Living and Dying...238
Lost........................149
Love....................133, 278, 292, 293
Lovers....................287
Lust................282, 283

M

Majority.............37, 38
Man.......................230
Mankind..................51
Married..................272
Mind....................184, 193, 206, 207
Miracles.................252
Money....................27, 40, 174
Moonlight..............178
Morning................107
Mountain...............176
Music..............46, 265
Myself...............2, 263

N

Nature...................105, 127, 144, 155, 261
News.......................18
November..............179

O

Opportunity............254
Owls......................180

P

Peace of mind........229
Prejudices..................6
Philosophers..............7, 8, 142
Points-of-view.......124

Poetry..............72, 196
Poverty............17, 134
Power......................45
Purified................285

R

Reason...................268
Reflection(s)..204, 248
Rhythms................219
Romance...............288

S

Seasons..................189
Secret(s)...............214, 237, 281
Senses....................245
Silence...................215
Simplicity...............52, 89, 95
Sincerity................191
Society....................68
Solitude...................22
Soul...............216, 228
Spring...................126, 147, 148
Stars......................222
Streams.................267
Strength...................47
Summer................101
Summer Days........195
Sympathy..............290
System....................74

298 /

T

Tea......................208
Think...................182
Thinker................177
Thought(s)............53, 60, 194, 243
Time......................4, 99, 102, 106, 251
Tools......................11
Transcendentalist...145
Truth...................135, 138, 210, 218, 224

U

Universe................130

V

Veneration.............291
Virtue..............48, 235
Vote.......................34

W

Waiting..................170
Walk....................139, 175, 220, 258
War........................33
Water...................117, 151, 199, 242
Wealth.............56, 157
Western skies.........275
Wider views...........201
Winds...................253
Wilderness.............114
Wisdom.................231
Women..........273, 274
Woods..................122, 141, 181
Word(s)................100, 226, 294
World...................250

Y

Year...............125, 154

/ 299

Bibliography

Thoreau, Henry David. *The Writings of Henry David Thoreau: Journal II, 1850, September 15, 1851*. vol. 2. 1906. ed. Bradford Torrey. New York: AMS Press, 1968

Thoreau, Henry David. *The Writings of Henry David Thoreau: Excursions and Poems*. vol. 5. 1906. New York: AMS Press, 1968.

Thoreau, Henry David. *The Writings of Henry David Thoreau: Journal I, 1837-1846*. vol. 7. 1906. ed. Bradford Torrey. New York: AMS Press, 1968.

Thoreau, Henry David. *The Writings of Henry David Thoreau: Walden*. Vol. 2. 1906. New York: AMS Press, 1968.

Thoreau, Henry David. *The Writings of Henry David Thoreau: Journal II, March 5-November 30, 1853*. vol. 11. 1906. ed. Bradford Torrey. New York: AMS Press, 1968.

Thoreau, Henry David. *The Writings of Henry David Thoreau: Cape Cod and Miscellanies*. vol 4. 1906. New York: AMS Press, 1968.

Thoreau, Henry David. *The Writings of Henry David Thoreau: Familiar Letters and Index*. vol. 6. 1906. ed. F.B. Sanborn. New York: AMS Press, 1968.

Thoreau, Henry David. *The Writings of Henry David Thoreau: Journal III, September 16, 1851 - April 30, 1852*. vol 9. 1906. ed. Bradford Torrey. New York: AMS Press, 1968.

Thoreau, Henry David. *The Writings of Henry David Thoreau: Journal X, August 8, 1857-June 29, 1858*. vol. 16. 1906. ed. Bradford Torrey. New York: AMS Press, 1968.

Acknowledgments

I would like to first and foremost thank my family. Your love and support will never be forgotten:

My mother Joan Luck, Kim and Chris Kostelnik, Donna and Nicolas Hughes, Josephine Kimek, Jack and Janice Klimek and Verna Burkowski.

None of this would be possible without my former professors and teachers who have influenced me more than they could ever imagine. For the many hours I have shared with them in the classroom, and for sculpting my intellectual life, I would like to thank:

Dr. Michael Foley, Dr. Thomas Jackson, Dr. Jay P. Clymer III, Dr. Alexander Vari, Professor Sandra Lewis, Mr. Leslie Nicholas, Mr. Mark Lemoncelli, Sr. Margaret Gannon, Mr. Haydn Gilmore, Mark Webber, Mr. Michael Freund and Dr. Sharon Nazarchuk.

I would like to thank my friends and acquaintances, for their unlimited kindness, and for their encouragement over the years. Your loyalty and love are beyond measure!

Thank you to: Phil Yurkon, Jessica Jellen, Ryan Ward, Michael Bennett and family, Michael C. Joziaitis, Nate Strand, Donna Robb & Bill Remington, Jim Ford, Jennifer Robb, Gordon and Sue West, Jack Bobinshot, Mark Bakos, Bill and Maria Vauter, Jenny Tigue, Dave Evans, Shelley and Steve Bartolomei, Sean Neary, Adam Gawat, Patrick Tindana, Andy Wanat, Mike Tomalis, Jack Shovlin and Jean Yeselavage.

Finally, a special thanks to Mike Lello and Nikki M. Mascali from *The Weekender*, the Marywood University Library, and the Thoreau Society.

Cover Painting

"Woodland Visitors *[by Nicholas P. Santoleri] is truly a print with a purpose. When you purchase this limited edition print you are supporting the Walden Woods Project while receiving a lasting reminder of the historic landscape you are helping to protect.*"

- Don Henley

The Walden Woods Project is a nonprofit organization founded in April 1990 by Don Henley (Grammy Award-Winning recording artist and member of the Eagles) to preserve the historic and environmentally sensitive land near Walden Pond in Concord, Massachusetts. Parcels of historic Walden Woods surrounding Walden Pond, the famed retreat of Henry David Thoreau, were threatened by the development of condominiums and an office park.

Each print has been individually hand signed by the artist and one of these celebrities: Kirstie Alley, Jimmy Buffett, Whoopi Goldberg, Tom Hanks, Don Henley, Bette Midler, and Jack Nicholson. Each print is individually numbered and comes with a certificate of authenticity signed by the artist and a thank-you letter from The Walden Woods Project.

The edition is limited to 2,500 prints. Each image is 11.25" x 22.5" in size. The issue price is $200.00. For more information, call (610) 995-2047 or visit www.santoleri.com.